How Are They Made?
Guitars

Wendy Blaxland

Marshall Cavendish
Benchmark

New York

This edition first published in 2010 in the United States of America by
MARSHALL CAVENDISH BENCHMARK
An imprint of Marshall Cavendish Corporation

Website: www.marshallcavendish.us

This publication represents the opinions and views of the author based on Wendy Blaxland's personal experience, knowledge, and research. The information in this book serves as a general guide only. The author and publisher have used their best efforts in preparing this book and disclaim liability rising directly and indirectly from the use and application of this book.

Other Marshall Cavendish Offices:
Marshall Cavendish Ltd. 5th Floor, 32-38 Saffron Hill, London EC1N 8 FH, UK • Marshall Cavendish International (Asia) Private Limited, 1 New Industrial Road, Singapore 536196 • Marshall Cavendish International (Thailand) Co Ltd. 253 Asoke, 12th Flr, Sukhumvit 21 Road, Klongtoey Nua, Wattana, Bangkok 10110, Thailand • Marshall Cavendish (Malaysia) Sdn Bhd, Times Subang, Lot 46, Subang Hi-Tech Industrial Park, Batu Tiga, 40000 Shah Alam, Selangor Darul Ehsan, Malaysia

Marshall Cavendish is a trademark of Times Publishing Limited

All websites were available and accurate when this book was sent to press.

Library of Congress Cataloging-in-Publication Data

Blaxland, Wendy.
    Guitars / Wendy Blaxland.
        p. cm. — (How are they made?)
    Includes index.
    Summary: "Discusses how guitars are made"—Provided by publisher.
    ISBN 978-0-7614-4754-2
    1. Guitar--Construction—Juvenile literature. I. Title.
    ML1015.G9B57 2011
787.87'1923--dc22
                                            2009039880

First published in 2010 by
MACMILLAN EDUCATION AUSTRALIA PTY LTD
15–19 Claremont Street, South Yarra 3141

Visit our website at www.macmillan.com.au or go directly to www.macmillanlibrary.com.au

Associated companies and representatives throughout the world.

Edited by Anna Fern
Text and cover design by Cristina Neri, Canary Graphic Design
Page layout by Peggy Bampton, Relish Graphic
Photo research by Jes Senbergs
Map by Damien Demaj, DEMAP; modified by Cristina Neri, Canary Graphic Design

Printed in the United States

Acknowledgments
The author would like to thank the following for their expert advice: Dick Boak, The Martin Guitar Company, Nazareth, Pennsylvania, United States; Rick Falkiner, guitar expert, Sydney, Australia; and Gregory Pikler, Lecturer in Guitar, Sydney Conservatorium, Australia.

The author and the publisher are grateful to the following for permission to reproduce copyright material:

Front cover photographs: Red and white electric guitar, Pixhook/istockphoto (top right); orange and red electric guitar, Pixhook/istockphoto (top left); black acoustic guitar, © Sharon Dominick/istockphoto (bottom left); acoustic guitar, Pixhook/istockphoto (bottom right).

Photographs courtesy of:
Elnur Amikishiyev/iStockphoto, **22**; Ernie Ball, **19**; *The Guitar Player*, c. 1672 (oil on canvas), Vermeer, Jan (1632–75)/The Iveagh Bequest, Kenwood House, London, UK/The Bridgeman Art Library, **6**; © Sally A. Morgan, Ecoscene/Corbis, **14**; © Eric Luse, *San Francisco Chronicle*/Corbis, **16**; © Lawrence Manning/Corbis, **5**; © Michael Ochs Archives/Corbis, **7**; © Gry Baz/Dreamstimes, **30**; Fender, **20**, **24**; Steve Catlin/Getty Images, **10**; Hayley Madden/Getty Images, **11** (right); Donald Miralle/Getty Images, **25**; Workbook Stock/Getty Images, **17** (right); Expoited Fairy/iStockphoto, **26**; Pixhook/iStockphoto, **3** (right), **3** (left), **8** (right), **11** (left), **17** (left), **21** (bottom); Rapid Eye/iStockphoto, **4**; Wave 720/iStockphoto, **8** (left); © Ace Stock Limited/Alamy/Photolibrary, **29**; © Paul Collis/Alamy/Photolibrary, **9**; © David Pearson/Alamy/Photolibrary, **23**; © The Stock Asylum, LLC/Alamy/Photolibrary, **27**; © Timothy O'Keefe/Photolibrary, **28**; © Kim Steele/Photolibrary, **21** (top); Reuters/Picture Media/Jean-Paul Pelissier, **18**.

While every care has been taken to trace and acknowledge copyright, the publisher tenders their apologies for any accidental infringement where copyright has proved untraceable. Where the attempt has been unsuccessful, the publisher welcomes information that would redress the situation.

1 3 5 6 4 2

Contents

Glossary Words

When a word is printed in **bold**, you can look up its meaning in the Glossary on page 31.

From Raw Materials to Products

Everything we use is made from raw materials from Earth. These are called natural resources. People take natural resources and make them into useful products.

Guitars

Guitars are stringed instruments, usually played by plucking or strumming. They may be **acoustic** or electric. An acoustic guitar has a hollow wooden body, which makes the sound produced by the strings louder. An electric guitar usually has a solid body. The sound of an electric guitar is made louder by plugging the guitar into an electric **amplifier** and a speaker.

The main raw materials used to make guitars are wood and steel. Hollow-bodied guitars are constructed from different types of wood, with the strings and fittings made of steel. Classical acoustic guitars use nylon strings, too. Solid electric guitar bodies are usually made of wood, or sometimes other materials such as plastic.

Guitar shape varies, but most are curved with a narrower waist in the middle.

Why Do We Need Guitars?

Guitars are a vital part of many musical styles, such as classical guitar, **flamenco**, jazz, country music, and rock. Players can accompany their own singing, or be part of a band. The basics are easy to learn, and acoustic guitars can be carried and played anywhere.

Guitars vary widely. They usually have six strings, but may have as few as four or as many as twelve strings. Guitars may be *guitarrons* larger than cellos, or tiny *requintos* half the size of an ordinary guitar. Their sounds range from contrabass guitars, an **octave** lower than regular guitars, to soprano guitars, an octave higher.

Guitar bands rehearse in garages everywhere.

Guess What!

The word *guitar* comes from the Spanish *guitarra*. This developed from the Arabic *quitara* and Latin *cithara*, which stems from the Greek word *kithara*, which in turn may come from the Persian *sihtar*, related to the Indian instrument the sitar.

5

The History of Guitars

Guitars are similar to stringed instruments played five thousand years ago. Their clearest ancestors, however, are the Spanish *vihuela* and *guiterra*, from the 1400s. By 1800, the modern guitar with six strings appeared. In the 1900s advances, such as steel strings, amplifying sounds with electricity, and recorded music, meant guitars became popular worldwide.

This painting from around 1672 by the Dutch painter Vermeer shows a woman playing a vihuela.

Guitars through the Ages

700s CE
Moors from northwest Africa bring the four-string *oud* when they conquer the Iberian Peninsula (now Spain and Portugal).

1400s–1500s
The Spanish *vihuela* is played by court ladies in Spain and France. Common people play the *guiterra.*

1833
The Martin Guitar Company is founded in New York.

700 CE

1200

1400

1500

1800

1200
The *oud* develops into both the round-backed Moorish guitar and the modern-looking Latin guitar.

1546
The first guitar music is published.

1800
The modern six-string guitar appears with six single strings, replacing five double strings.

1840
Spanish guitarist and luthier Antonio de Torres establishes the shape, design, and construction of the modern classical guitar.

Les Paul, the electric guitar pioneer, in his garage studio.

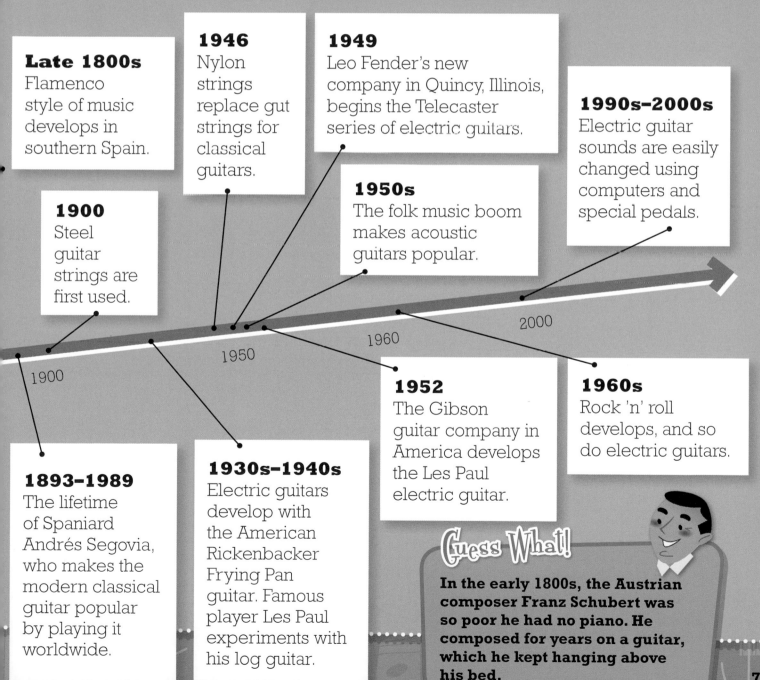

Late 1800s
Flamenco style of music develops in southern Spain.

1946
Nylon strings replace gut strings for classical guitars.

1949
Leo Fender's new company in Quincy, Illinois, begins the Telecaster series of electric guitars.

1990s–2000s
Electric guitar sounds are easily changed using computers and special pedals.

1900
Steel guitar strings are first used.

1950s
The folk music boom makes acoustic guitars popular.

1900

1950

1960

2000

1952
The Gibson guitar company in America develops the Les Paul electric guitar.

1960s
Rock 'n' roll develops, and so do electric guitars.

1893–1989
The lifetime of Spaniard Andrés Segovia, who makes the modern classical guitar popular by playing it worldwide.

1930s–1940s
Electric guitars develop with the American Rickenbacker Frying Pan guitar. Famous player Les Paul experiments with his log guitar.

Guess What!

In the early 1800s, the Austrian composer Franz Schubert was so poor he had no piano. He composed for years on a guitar, which he kept hanging above his bed.

What are Guitars Made From?

Guitars with hollow bodies are made from different types of wood. The solid bodies of electric guitars are usually made from wood, too, but sometimes other materials such as plastic and graphite are also used.

Strings are made of steel or nylon. The steel from which guitar strings and other parts are made is an **alloy**, or mixture. It contains about 95 percent iron and up to one percent carbon, with a little manganese and silicon.

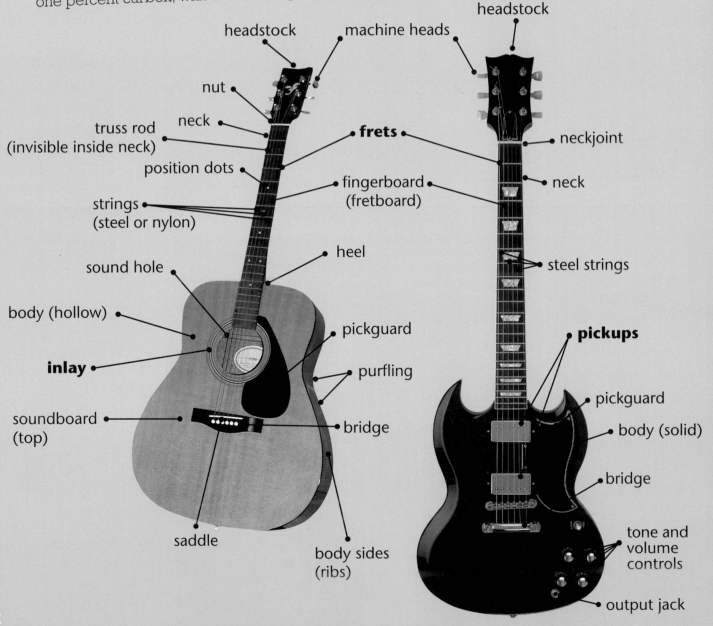

headstock

machine heads

headstock

nut

neck

frets

neckjoint

truss rod
(invisible inside neck)

position dots

fingerboard
(fretboard)

neck

strings
(steel or nylon)

heel

steel strings

sound hole

body (hollow)

pickguard

pickups

inlay

purfling

pickguard

soundboard
(top)

bridge

body (solid)

bridge

saddle

body sides
(ribs)

tone and
volume
controls

output jack

Materials

Many different materials are used to make guitars. As with the making of all products, energy is also used to run the machines that mine and harvest the raw materials, make the metals, timber, and plastic, and construct the guitars.

Materials Used to Make Guitars

Material	Purpose and Qualities
Wood (solid, pieced together, or layered)	Used for bodies and necks, especially of acoustic guitars. Wood is beautiful, amplifies sounds, and gives rich tones.
Stainless steel	Used for strings, fittings, frets, and electric parts of guitars.
Other metals (bronze, copper, aluminum alloys)	Used in strings, frets, and fittings.
Graphite	Sometimes used for solid electric guitar bodies.
Bone, plastic compounds	Medium-hard materials for nuts and saddles.
Mother-of-pearl, gems, precious metals	Used for beautiful decorative inlays.
Silk	Used with steel in the core of special acoustic guitar strings.
Nylon	Used in strings for classical acoustic guitars.
Fillers, sealers, stains	Used to fill, seal, or color wood.
Lacquers, polyurethane plastic	Used for finishing and to protect guitar bodies.
Glues (animal or plastic resin)	Hold guitar parts together.

Plastic is used for pickguards.

Guitar Design

Guitars vary greatly in design. Acoustic guitars are usually more traditionally shaped. Electric guitars thrive on new advances in technology. Guitars range from cheap, mass-produced instruments to very expensive, elaborately decorated guitars made of rare woods or sleek **synthetic** materials.

Guitars are played by individuals who choose a guitar designed for their type of music, such as classical, flamenco, country, or heavy metal, and for their style of playing, from delicate to heavy, solo, or in a band. The large, loud, electric Dreadnought suits rhythm players and accompanying singers. Smaller guitars are good for strumming or finger-plucking techniques.

Electric guitars put developing technology to use, as designers and players test new ideas together. A recent guitar has a built-in MP3 player, acts like a studio to record sounds, can download music to a computer, and can even teach its owner how to play.

Guess What!

One electric guitar changed color as it was played. Lights of different colors within its clear plastic body linked to the different musical notes.

This electro-acoustic guitar features an unusual sound hole design.

Design Choices

The first design choice is which material to use. Harder woods produce brighter sounds, and softer woods produce mellower, softer sounds. Solid-bodied guitars can also be made of polycarbonate plastic or even glass. With easily **molded** plastic, the choice of guitar shapes is endless.

Designers must also choose between types of glue. Guitars held with glues made from animal skins are easier to take apart for repairs or changes. Synthetic glues are stronger and won't damage the guitar by absorbing moisture or allowing decay.

Decoration is another design choice, from plain to exquisite decorations around the soundhole, and on the fingerboard, headstock, or entire body. Decorative materials include mother-of-pearl, various woods, stamped or carved metal, and even fabric. The **logo** of the **manufacturer** is often inlaid into the headstock.

Famous guitarists, such as Bruce Springsteen, often play custom-made or limited edition guitars.

From Wood and Steel to Guitars

The process of making everyday objects such as guitars from raw materials involves many steps. In the first stage, the timber and stainless steel are prepared. The guitar body and strings are made in the second stage. In the final stage, fittings and strings are added before the guitar is tuned and tried out.

Question & Answer

What is a guitarron?

A guitarron is a large bass guitar used in Mexican mariachi bands.

Stage 1: Making Guitar Materials

Wood

The timber for the guitar is sawn to the right size.

↓

For hollow-bodied guitars, thin planks are glued together to make the wood for the top and back. For solid electric guitars, planks are cut to the right thickness.

↓

For guitar necks, wood is glued into blocks.

Steel

For guitar strings, iron and other metal **ores** are mined.

↓

Next, the iron is made into stainless steel.

↓

Then the steel is squeezed into long, thin wires.

Stage 2: Shaping Guitars

For hollow-bodied guitars, the guitar top and back are cut out.

⬇

The soundhole is cut in the top and a decorative **rosette** added to protect it.

⬇

Next, **bracings** are glued to the top and back and carved.

⬇

Now strips of wood for the guitar sides are joined together.

⬇

Next, linings are glued into the guitar sides and the top and back glued to them.

Solid electric guitar bodies are carved out of a block of wood.

To make steel strings, a wire core is covered with wrap wire on a string-winding machine.

Nylon strings are made by pushing melted nylon through small holes.

Stage 3: Finishing Guitars

The neck is cut to shape and a metal truss rod glued in.

⬇

Then the fingerboard is made.

⬇

Frets are glued in and machine heads added.

⬇

Next, the neck is attached to the guitar body.

⬇

The guitar body is stained, sealed, lacquered, and polished.

⬇

The bridge, headstock nut, saddle, and pins are attached.

⬇

Pickups and control knobs are attached to electric guitars.

⬇

Finally, the guitar is strung and tuned.

Raw Materials for Guitars

Making guitars involves a variety of natural and synthetic materials. These are combined to make instruments that can look and sound very different.

The most important raw material for making guitars is wood. Traditionally, **hardwoods** from trees up to eight hundred years old are used, because they are **flexible**, wide enough, even-grained, and strong. Many grow in South American and Asian rain forests. Timber from these trees is now scarce and very expensive. Guitar makers need to look at different woods and consider new ways of using wood.

Timber such as cedar takes a long time to grow and is expensive.

Canada 🌲 🎸

NORTH AMERICA

United States of America 🌲 ▲ ✛ 🎸

Mexico 🎸

ATLANTIC OCEAN

Brazil 🌲 🌀

SOUTH AMERICA

Argentina ✛

Steel and Synthetics

The steel from which guitar strings and other parts are made contains about 95 percent iron. While iron ore is found in certain countries, the steel **refineries** are usually elsewhere.

Synthetics such as nylon, glues, and lacquers used in making guitars are made from oil and gas produced by the **petrochemical industry**. Major petrochemical producers are found in the United States, western Europe, the Middle East, and Asia.

This map shows countries that are important to the production of guitars.

Guess What!

More than forty kinds of wood can be used to make guitars. They include spruce from Germany, cedar from Canada, and rosewood from Brazil and India.

Key

- 🌲 Important timber-producing countries
- ⊗ Important iron-ore–mining countries
- ▲ Important stainless-steel–manufacturing countries
- ✛ Important guitar-string–producing countries
- 🎸 Important guitar-manufacturing countries

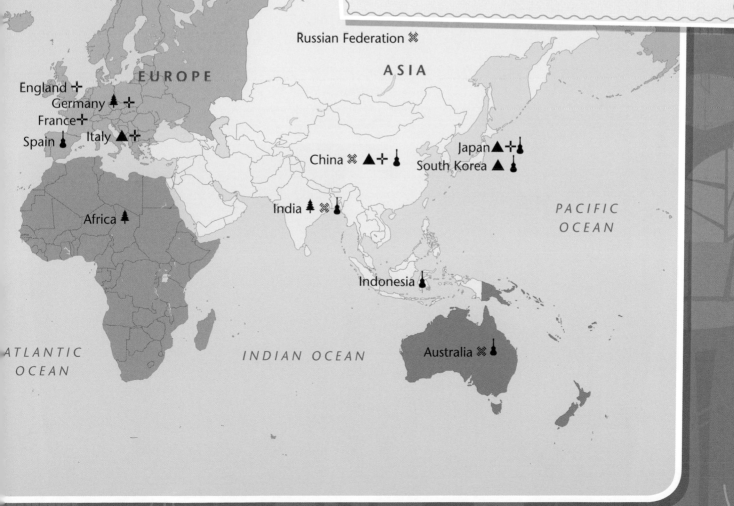

Stage 1: Making Guitar Materials

The timber for guitars is chosen carefully because it affects the way they look and sound. Soundboards for acoustic folk guitars are traditionally made of lightweight spruce and cedar, which vibrate well. The backs are made of harder rosewood, mahogany, or maple. Electric guitars are often made of mahogany, ash, or alder.

Preparing the Wood

First, planks are sawn to the right length. Usually two planks must be joined to provide the width of a guitar. Hollow-bodied guitars use much thinner wood for the front, back, and sides than solid electric guitar bodies. The planks of hollow-bodied guitars are joined by gluing a thin strip of wood behind the joints. Planks for solid-bodied guitars are cut to the right thickness, dried, glued, and clamped together.

Guitar necks are made from strong woods, either in a solid piece or several blocks glued together. Sometimes a veneer or thin layer of more beautiful wood is glued over a less attractive solid wood.

A luthier taps a piece of redwood to see if it sounds right for the guitar he will make.

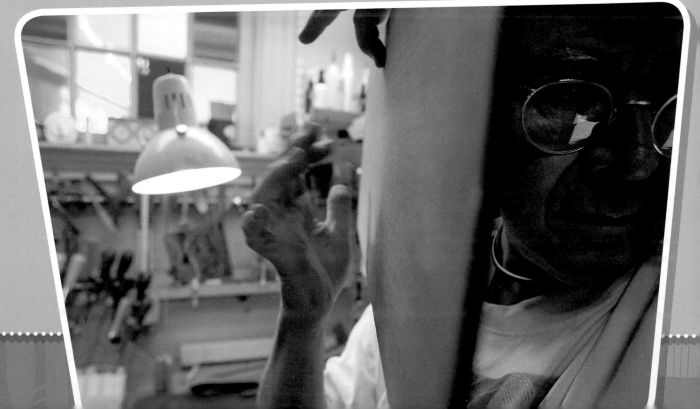

Stainless Steel

Iron and the other metals used to make guitar parts are first mined from the ground as ore. The ore is **smelted** in a hot **furnace** to extract the iron. Then carbon, scrap stainless steel, and other metals such as nickel and chromium are added to make the iron into stainless steel. Stainless steel is used to make strings, frets, machine heads, and truss rods for guitars.

Red-hot molten steel will cool and harden into bars.

Guess What!

In the 1800s in Spain, Francisco Tarrega was the first guitar player to play a guitar by plucking with his fingernails. He could also play beautifully with his left hand while smoking a cigar with his right!

Preparing Wire for Strings

The stainless steel used for guitar strings contains a large amount of carbon. The **molten** steel is poured into molds to make rectangular steel bars. The bars are then run through a mill where hot rollers squeeze the metal into thinner, longer rods. Next the steel rods are drawn through a series of holes. The holes get smaller till the wire is thin enough. During this process the wire is carefully heated and cooled to make it soft and easier to work.

Stage 2: Shaping Guitars

For a hollow guitar, the top and back are cut out with power tools. Next, the soundhole is cut in the top, and a decorative rosette glued around it for support.

Wide, thin wooden strips for the guitar sides are soaked and heated, bent by pressing them to the chosen curves, then connected by wooden blocks. Notched wooden linings are then glued and clamped inside the side strips to support the top and back.

Next, bracings are carved and glued to the top and back. The sides are glued to the top and back and a protective binding put on the guitar edges. The guitar is then sanded smooth, and sprayed with many coats of polyurethane lacquer. Lastly, a carefully angled hole is cut so the neck can be joined in.

Solid wooden electric guitar bodies may be carved out by hand or by machine, often computerized. Then they are sanded smooth. Next, metal fixtures are added for joining on the neck and supporting electric devices.

The curved wooden sides of the guitar are shaped by soaking the wood and pressing it against curved wooden blocks.

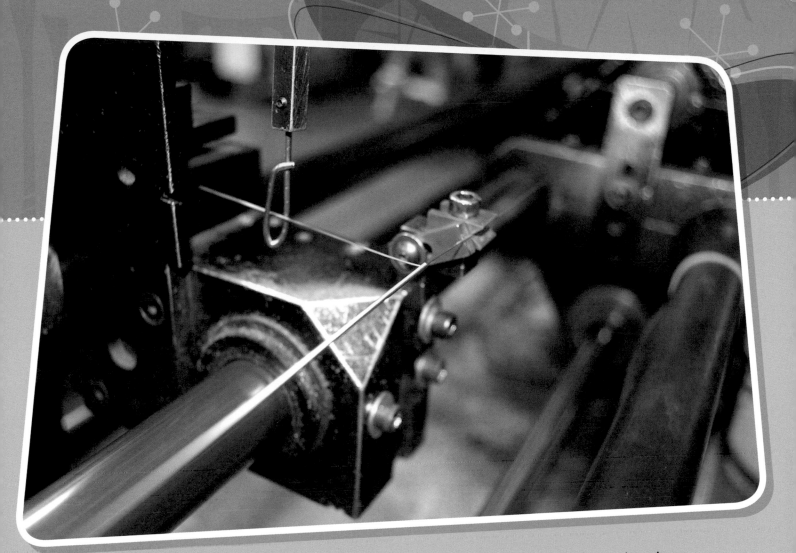

Strings are essential to make a guitar sing.

Question & Answer

What were guitar strings made from before steel strings were used?

Animal guts! Cleaned lamb intestines were twisted together on a winder, stretched on a frame, bleached, dried, and sanded smooth. Lastly the strings were oiled.

Making Guitar Strings

Most guitar strings have steel cores, often coated by slippery metals such as nickel. Coils of other metals, such as brass, bronze, copper, or nickel, may be tightly wound around the core to make different sounds. For instance, wire wound with nickel gives electric guitar strings a bright sound.

To make steel strings, the ball or anchor end of the core wire is fastened to a string-winding machine. The machine then spins to wrap the core wire tightly with outer wire.

Classical guitars are usually partly strung with smooth, inexpensive nylon strings. The three strings that make high notes, however, are just made of nylon. Molten nylon is pushed through small holes to make thread for strings. The strings that make lower notes are made of silk or nylon wrapped with silver-alloy wire.

Stage 3: Finishing Guitars

Now the guitar neck is made and joined to the body.

Making the Guitar Neck

First, the glued wooden neck block is carved out with power tools. A metal truss rod is glued into a groove in the neck to add strength and keep the neck straight.

Next, the fingerboard is made of thin wood and glued over the truss rod. Grooves are cut for the metal frets, which are hammered, pressed, or glued in. Then the machine heads are added to stretch the strings so they can make the proper sounds. Finally, the neck is bolted or glued onto the guitar body.

Metal frets are glued onto the fingerboard.

Guess What!

José, a Portuguese luthier, took nine months to build the world's biggest guitar. The guitar is 199.5 feet (60.8 meters) long and people can actually climb inside it.

Electrical fittings are added to electric guitars so that they can be plugged into amplifiers.

The Final Touches

The guitar body may now be sprayed with lacquer, buffed, and polished to a fine finish. For acoustic guitars, a wooden bridge with precisely drilled holes is glued on the top. This anchors the strings and transfers their sound to the hollow wooden guitar body to make it louder. Next the headstock nut, a bar made of hard plastic or bone, is glued on. It separates and guides the strings coming from the machine heads. The saddle and pins are added too.

Electric guitars need electric fittings. A jack or cable fitting and mini-microphones called pickups transfer the strings' sounds to an amplifier and speakers. Volume and tone knobs may also be added, and a lever-operated tremolo bar for quivering sound effects.

Now the guitar can finally be strung, tuned, and played. It takes from ten days to nine months or more to make a guitar.

Packaging and Distribution

Products are packaged to protect them while they are being transported. Packaging also shows the maker's brand and makes products look attractive when they are displayed for sale.

Guitars are large, fragile musical instruments. They must be packaged carefully to prevent damage from changes in temperature and humidity, since wood absorbs water from the air. Airtight plastic bags keep the water content in the air around each guitar steady. Then they are packed carefully into cartons, often separated by bubble wrap or packing peanuts. Guitars generally hang in stores unpackaged because buyers want to look at, touch, and play them.

Musicians often keep their guitars in special protective cases. These range from soft padded plastic bags to harder, specially shaped cases. Touring musicians protect electric guitars in hard-shell rectangular cases. Guitar cases may advertise guitar brands.

When traveling, musicians carry their guitars in hard protective cases.

Music stores display guitars so buyers can touch and play them.

Distribution

Inexpensive beginners' guitars can be bought from chain stores. Electric guitars are often sold packaged with an amplifier, tuner, power cord, plectrum for plucking the strings, and music lessons. More expensive guitars may be sold directly to professional musicians.

Big factories make thousands of guitars and ship them to other countries. Guitars may be sold to **distributors** who sell them to **retailers** in department stores and specialist guitar stores. Guitars can also be sold through catalogs and over the Internet. Many guitars are sold second-hand, in stores, auctions, or on websites run by fans of certain guitar styles.

Guess What!

Each new country in the guitar industry has learned from the experience of others. The first large guitar factories were in the United States. The Japanese copied these, at first making low-quality guitars. Now Japanese guitars are excellent. Today, Chinese guitar manufacturers are building on lessons from the United States, Japan, Korea, and Indonesia.

23

Marketing and Advertising

Marketing and advertising are used to promote and sell products.

Marketing

Guitar companies work closely with popular musicians to market their instruments. Sometimes they even name instruments after great guitarists, such as the Gibson Les Paul. Companies may also sponsor musicians, who in turn advertise their guitars.

Guitars play a major part in marketing the huge worldwide entertainment industry. They help make the music that plays in television commercials, drifts through elevators, throbs from car radios, and tempts people to dance. The driving energy of electric guitars has helped make musicians megastars. With satellite linkups, guitars being played at concerts happening in one place can be seen and heard worldwide.

Question & Answer

What is the world's most expensive guitar?

A Fender Stratocaster guitar signed by many famous musicians, including Paul McCartney, sold for $2.7 million at an auction to raise money for charity in 2005.

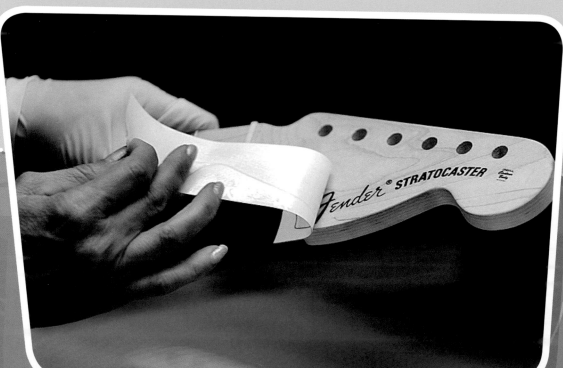

Fender Stratocaster guitars have been used by many famous lead guitarists.

24

Advertising

Guitars are easy to learn to play and lots of people enjoy playing their favorite songs on their own guitars. As their playing improves, they want better guitars or guitars with a particular sound, and they often save to buy their next guitar.

Advances in manufacturing technology mean that guitars are inexpensive to buy. New guitars are advertised in print and online catalogs, music and special guitar magazines. Second-hand guitars and older **vintage** guitars can be advertised locally, at auctions, and online.

Part of the image of many megastars is their choice of guitar.

Production of Guitars

Products can be made in factories in huge quantities. This is called mass production. They may also be made in small quantities by hand, by skilled craftspeople.

Mass Production

Most guitars are made by machines in factories. Some are huge complexes with hundreds of employees who may have no real interest in guitars, usually repeating one part of the process. These factories can produce enormous numbers of guitars.

Guitars are also made in factories that pride themselves on having knowledgeable craftspeople, often guitar players themselves. They may specialize in one part of the process, but understand it all. These craftspeople can build a variety of guitars, from cheaper acoustic guitars, to those made specifically to a customer's own design.

Mass-produced electric guitar bodies wait for the next stage of their assembly.

This luthier is filing the neck for the guitar in which he has glued bracing.

Small-Scale Production

Guitar players often develop a strong relationship with their instruments, so choosing the right guitar is very important. Trying different guitars helps players find the one they like best. Some can afford a custom-built guitar from a well-known company. Others prefer dealing with an individual luthier they trust.

Luthiers need a great deal of skill and experience to produce good handmade guitars. Many countries, such as the United States, Australia, Spain, and Portugal, have fine traditions of small guitar workshops.

Some people decide to build their own guitars. Guitar-making courses can guide them through the process. Information is also available in books and on the Internet.

Guitars and the Environment

Making any product affects the environment. It also has an effect on the people who make the product. It is important to think about the impact of a product through its entire life cycle. This includes getting the raw materials, making the product, and disposing of it. Any problems need to be worked on so products can be made in the best ways possible.

Materials

Wood is a **renewable resource**, but traditional guitar-making hardwoods are running out. Using **sustainable** timber may mean finding processes that use wood from faster-growing or younger, thinner trees.

Mining iron and making steel uses large amounts of energy. Mining may disturb animals and plants, and pollute air and water. Nylon and other synthetic materials used in making guitars come from oil and gas, which will eventually run out. Dangers to workers include mine collapses, factory noise, and fumes.

Manufacturing guitars can affect the environment and the people who make them.

Older and unusual guitars are treasured by collectors.

Recycling

Guitars are perfect for reusing and recycling. A well-built and cared-for guitar can be sold or given away. Vintage or older guitars may be very valuable. Damaged guitars can often be repaired, and, if fastened with animal glues, they can easily be taken apart. Electric guitars, too, can be repaired and renewed.

Guitar strings need to be replaced frequently, depending on how often and how hard they are played. They lose their tone and stretchiness, and sweat from guitar players' fingers reacts with the metals to destroy them. However, metals in guitar strings are generally valuable and can be recycled. Old strings can be reused to hang pictures and string jewelry.

Guess What!

An Australian company made a pair of guitar picks from African meteorites about 4 billion years old. They cost more than $3,900.

Questions to Think About

What sort of music do you play on your guitar?

We need to conserve the raw materials used to produce even ordinary objects such as guitars. Recycling materials such as stainless steel, conserving energy, and preventing pollution as much as possible means there will be enough resources in the future and a cleaner environment.

These are some questions you might like to think about:

✽ How many types of music can you think of where guitars are used?

✽ How can used guitar strings be recycled?

✽ Find pictures of the most unusual guitars you can. Why are they designed this way?

✽ How can the scarcity of timber for guitar-making be solved?

✽ Listen to some guitar music. What are some differences between music from acoustic and electric guitars?

✽ Design your own ideal guitar, or a carrying case for a particular guitar. What qualities does it need?

Glossary

acoustic
A type of instrument whose sound is made louder by vibrating within its wooden body.

alloy
A material made from a mixture of metals.

amplifier
An electronic device that makes sounds louder.

bracings
Pieces that add strength.

distributors
Sellers of large quantities of goods that have the right to sell a particular product in a certain area.

fillers
Substances used to fill gaps and cracks.

flamenco
Rhythmic Spanish gypsy dance music.

flexible
Able to bend.

frets
Metal bars under a guitar's strings that help the player find the right note.

furnace
A very hot oven.

hardwoods
Trees that have broad leaves and produce fruit, such as oak and maple.

inlay
A decoration set into a material so that the surface remains smooth.

logo
Image that represents a company brand.

manufacturer
Maker, usually in a factory.

molten
Heated into a liquid.

molded
Made into objects by being poured into a hollow shape called a mold.

octave
A group of eight musical notes.

ores
Minerals or rocks containing metal.

petrochemical industry
Manufacturers that make chemical products such as plastic from petroleum oil and natural gas.

pickup
A device that picks up the sound from a guitar and transfers it to an electric amplifier that will make the sound louder.

refineries
Factories where raw materials are treated to make them purer or more useful.

renewable resource
Resource that can be easily grown or made again.

retailers
Stores that sell products to individual customers.

rosette
A decorative circular band surrounding a guitar's sound hole.

smelted
Melted to separate metallic elements.

sustainable
Able to be continued without hurting the environment in the long term.

synthetic
Made by humans, often using petrochemicals.

vintage
High-quality items from a particular time or fashion era.